The European Union

Union

Political, Social, and Economic Cooperation

The
EUROPEAN UNION

POLITICAL, SOCIAL, AND ECONOMIC COOPERATION

The European Union

Political, Social, and Economic Cooperation

SLOVENIA

by
Heather Docalavich

Mason Crest Publishers
Philadelphia

Mason Crest Publishers Inc.
370 Reed Road, Broomall, Pennsylvania 19008
(866) MCP-BOOK (toll free)
www.masoncrest.com

First printing
1 2 3 4 5 6 7 8 9 10

Library of Congress Cataloging-in-Publication Data

Docalavich, Heather.
  Slovenia / by Heather Docalavich.
      p. cm.—(The European Union: political, social, and economic cooperation)
  Includes index.
    ISBN 1-4222-0061-2
    ISBN 1-4222-0038-8 (series)
  1. European Union—Slovenia—Juvenile literature. 2. Slovenia—Juvenile literature. I. Title. II. European Union (Series) (Philadelphia, Pa.)
  DR1360.D63 2006
  949.7303—dc22
                           2005012751

Produced by Harding House Publishing Service, Inc.
www.hardinghousepages.com
Interior design by Benjamin Stewart.
Cover design by MK Bassett-Harvey.
Printed in the Hashemite Kingdom of Jordan.

CONTENTS

THE
EUROPEAN
UNION

GREENLAND SEA

BARENTS SEA

ICELAND
Reykjavik

NORWEGIAN SEA

NORWAY
Oslo
Bergen
Lillehammer
Trondheim

SWEDEN
Stockholm
Gothenburg
Norrköping

DENMARK
Aalborg
Odense
Copenhagen
Malmö

UNITED KINGDOM
Edinburgh
Glasgow
Belfast
Liverpool
Manchester
Birmingham
London

IRELAND
Dublin
Cork
Killarney

North Sea
Irish Sea
St. George's Channel
English Channel

THE NETHERLANDS
Amsterdam
Rotterdam
The Hague

BELGIUM
Brussels

LUXEMBOURG
Luxembourg

GERMANY
Hamburg
Berlin
Cologne
Düsseldorf
Leipzig
Dresden
Frankfurt am Main
Stuttgart
Munich

FRANCE
Paris
Nantes
Bordeaux
Toulouse
Lyons
Marseille
Nice

SWITZERLAND
Bern
Geneva
Turin

Bay of Biscay

PORTUGAL
Porto
Lisbon
Faro

SPAIN
Vigo
Bilbao
Madrid
Barcelona
Valencia
Seville

Strait of Gibraltar

FINLAND
Tampere
Turku
Helsinki

Gulf of Bothnia
Gulf of Finland

RUSSIA
Moscow

ESTONIA
Tallinn
Tartu

LATVIA
Riga
Daugavpils

Gulf of Riga

LITHUANIA
Klaipeda
Kaunas
Vilnius

RUSSIA
Gdansk

BALTIC SEA

POLAND
Warsaw
Wroclaw
Kraków

BELARUS
Minsk

UKRAINE
Kyiv

CZECH REPUBLIC
Prague
Brno
Plzen

SLOVAKIA
Košice
Bratislava

AUSTRIA
Vienna
Linz
Salzburg

HUNGARY
Budapest
Györ
Szeged

MOLDOVA
Chisinau

Sea of Azov

SLOVENIA
Ljubljana

CROATIA
Zagreb
Rijeka

BOSNIA-HERCEGOVINA
Sarajevo

ITALY
Milan
Venice
Florence
Rome
Naples

YUGOSLAVIA
Belgrade

ROMANIA
Bucharest

BLACK SEA

BULGARIA
Sofia

MACEDONIA
Skopje

ALBANIA
Tirana

GREECE
Thessaloniki
Athens
Kalamata

ADRIATIC SEA
TYRRHENIAN SEA
IONIAN SEA
AEGEAN SEA
Sea of Crete

TURKEY
Ankara

CYPRUS
Lefkosia (Nicosia)
Lemesos

SYRIA

LEBANON
Damascus

JORDAN
Jerusalem
Amman

ISRAEL & THE PALESTINIAN TERRITORIES

MALTA
Valetta

MEDITERRANEAN SEA

MOROCCO
Rabat

ALGERIA
Algiers

TUNISIA
Tunis
Tripoli

LIBYA

EGYPT
Cairo

WHITE SEA

SLOVENIA
European Union Member since 2004

Murska Sobota

Dravograd

Maribor

Ptuj

Kranjska Gora

Jesenice

Polzela

Rogaška Slatina

Tolmin

Kranj

Celije

Škohja Loka

★ **Ljubljana**

Nova Gorica

Idrija

Krško

Brežice

Postonja

Cerknica

Novo Mesto

Koĉevje

Predgrad

INTRODUCTION

Sixty years ago, Europe lay scarred from the battles of the Second World War. During the next several years, a plan began to take shape that would unite the countries of the European continent so that future wars would be inconceivable. On May 9, 1950, French Foreign Minister Robert Schuman issued a declaration calling on France, Germany, and other European countries to pool together their coal and steel production as "the first concrete foundation of a European federation." "Europe Day" is celebrated each year on May 9 to commemorate the beginning of the European Union (EU).

The EU consists of twenty-five countries, spanning the continent from Ireland in the west to the border of Russia in the east. Eight of the ten most recently admitted EU member states are former communist regimes that were behind the Iron Curtain for most of the latter half of the twentieth century.

Any European country with a democratic government, a functioning market economy, respect for fundamental rights, and a government capable of implementing EU laws and policies may apply for membership. Bulgaria and Romania are set to join the EU in 2007. Croatia and Turkey have also embarked on the road to EU membership.

While the EU began as an idea to ensure peace in Europe through interconnected economies, it has evolved into so much more today:

- Citizens can travel freely throughout most of the EU without carrying a passport and without stopping for border checks.

- EU citizens can live, work, study, and retire in another EU country if they wish.

- The euro, the single currency accepted throughout twelve of the EU countries (with more to come), is one of the EU's most tangible achievements, facilitating commerce and making possible a single financial market that benefits both individuals and businesses.

- The EU ensures cooperation in the fight against cross-border crime and terrorism.

- The EU is spearheading world efforts to preserve the environment.

- As the world's largest trading bloc, the EU uses its influence to promote fair rules for world trade, ensuring that globalization also benefits the poorest countries.

- The EU is already the world's largest donor of humanitarian aid and development assistance, providing 55 percent of global official development assistance to developing countries in 2004.

The EU is neither a nation intended to replace existing nations, nor an international organization. The EU is unique—its member countries have established common institutions to which they delegate some of their sovereignty so that decisions on matters of joint interest can be made democratically at the European level.

Europe is a continent with many different traditions and languages, but with shared values such as democracy, freedom, and social justice, cherished values well known to North Americans. Indeed, the EU motto is "United in Diversity."

Enjoy your reading. Take advantage of this chance to learn more about Europe and the EU!

Ambassador John Bruton,
Head of Delegation of the European Commission, Washington, D.C.

Lake Bled, located north of Ljubljana, draws tourists to its picture-perfect vistas.
Bled Castle, located more than 300 feet above the lake, was the seat of regional bishops for 800 years.

CHAPTER 1

THE LANDSCAPE

Welcome to Slovenia, a small nation of amazing diversity. Nestled between the Alps of Austria and Italy, the plains of Hungary, and the sunny shores of the Adriatic Sea, Slovenia's 12,597 square miles (20,273 sq. kilometers) boast some of the most beautiful scenery in Central Europe.

One of the smallest nations in Europe, Slovenia is home to almost every type of geographic feature found in the rest of greater Europe. Diverse experiences await the adventurous visitor in Slovenia year round, whether your taste is skiing or snowboarding in the mountains, exploring the beauty and mystery of limestone caves and **thermal springs**, braving the rush of white-water canyons or sunbathing on warm sand, you can enjoy it all within less than three hours' drive. This has driven the explosive growth of Slovenian tourism, which has increased dramatically since Slovenia obtained its independence in 1991 from the former Yugoslavia.

MOUNTAINS, FORESTS, AND A SUN-DRENCHED COAST

Slovenia is heavily forested and terrain ranges from mountainous in the north, to flat in the coastal plains of the south. The more mountainous regions lend themselves to the grazing of livestock, while much of the rest of the land is **arable** and used for farming.

The Adriatic Sea provides not only important recreational opportunities and a lure for foreign tourists, but also access to other seaports for trade. Koper, Slovenia's only seaport, is an important trade center not only for Slovenia but also neighboring Austria, for whom it provides an important home for commercial ships.

The Alps in the north are renowned for their beauty and have been far less developed for tourism than those in neighboring Austria and Italy. The snow-capped peaks provide opportunities to pursue winter sports of all kinds, and

The island chapel in Lake Bled possesses the "bell of wishes," which supposedly grants all who ring it success in love.

Slovenia is home to the oldest recorded form of skiing in Europe. Backpackers enjoy more than 4,300 miles (6,920 kilometers) of marked foot trails through the mountains, an excellent way to explore the ancient forests and their wildlife.

RIVERS AND LAKES

The Slovenian countryside is dotted with lakes, rivers, and thermal springs. High in the mountains, *glacial lakes* disappear mysteriously under-

Northern Slovenia is dominated by the Alps, which are less developed than in other countries. Visitors can pursue recreation such as rock climbing, white-river rafting, and hiking.

ground at the beginning of each summer, only to emerge again in the fall. The runoff of melted mountain snow provides fresh water to Slovenia's major rivers, the Drava and the Sava, which run from the mountains to the seacoast and provide important irrigation and transport.

The limestone regions of the Karst plateau feature many dramatic rock formations, underground caves, and canyons. These areas are home to picturesque waterfalls and rapidly moving streams and rivers. Adventurous tourists take advantage of the natural surroundings to pursue activities like rock climbing, caving, and rafting.

Freshwater lakes also provide important fishing and recreation areas. Lake Bled and Lake Bohinj are the largest Slovenian lakes. In the coastal regions you can also find saltwater marshes and **tidal estuaries**. Based on the unique nature of the habitat they provide, the Secovlje Saltpans are protected as wetlands of international importance.

A Temperate Climate

Most of Slovenia has a **temperate** climate featuring warm summers and cool winters. Because of the **proximity** to the sea, the coastal area enjoys warmer Mediterranean weather, closer to that of its neighbors in Italy.

Average temperatures range from 28°F –2°C) in January to about 70°F (21°C) in July. The range is wider in the higher altitudes, while the seacoast enjoys warmer weather year round.

The northern, alpine region receives the heaviest precipitation, averaging 138 inches (350 centimeters) per year, much of it in the form of snow. The remaining areas of the country average about thirty-nine inches (100 centimeters) per year.

Trees, Plants, and Wildlife

About half of Slovenia is covered with woodlands. Most of the forests are in the north. While some of the forest cover is mixed, **deciduous** woodland, the primary forests are composed of **conifers** growing on higher altitudes. The Alpine region is also home to many different varieties of berries, wildflowers, and mushrooms.

Slovenian wildlife includes deer, **chamois**, hares, weasels, badgers, foxes, and lynx. The brown bear can be found in the mountains here. Birdwatchers have come to love this small country where hundreds of different migratory birds stop briefly in an easily covered area. Herring, cod, flounder, and a variety of other fish inhabit the coastal waters.

The country is also home to dozens of unique **indigenous** plants; the government has created two important national parks to protect its natural treasures. Strunjan Landscape Park is a protected tidal area, and Triglav National Park is one of the largest national parks in all of Europe.

This rich and varied landscape provides the backdrop for the nation's history and cultural heritage.

Slovenia, an independent nation for less than two decades, has a long history as a cultural region.

2 SLOVENIA'S HISTORY AND GOVERNMENT

Slovenia has only existed as an independent nation since 1991. For centuries, the area was more of a cultural region than a nation, passed back and forth between different ruling powers. Although the Slovenes have always possessed a strong sense of ethnic identity, the idea of a separate Slovenian state was not born until the **nationalist** movements of the late nineteenth century. At that time, Slovenian statehood was little more than a dream, and it took the developments of another hundred years to make

The rocky soil of Slovenia is a challenge to farm, but provides good pasture for the county's herds of cattle.

The borders of Slovenia today include the lands that have traditionally been the home of the Slovene people. Since Roman times, these lands have changed hands frequently, and borders and governments have shifted across the centuries. Today, Slovenia stands as a free, democratic country, one of the most prosperous of the new members of the European Union (EU). As a nation, Slovenia is committed to peace, prosperity, and developing new relationships with other countries. Slovenia, however, has come a long way to reach its current state.

EUROPEAN UNION—SLOVENIA

ANCIENT SLOVENIA

Ancient artifacts discovered on Slovene lands indicate the area was home to early human beings thousands of years ago. The **Celts** and the **Illyrians**, however, were the first recorded people of the territory. Around 100 BCE, the region came under Roman control and was governed under the provinces of Pannonia and Norricum.

By 600 CE, Slavic peoples fully inhabited the area, having migrated in waves from the East. A century later, a Frankish merchant named Samo united the people of the territory into the first recorded state. This early state collapsed shortly after Samo's death, and the area remained unstable until control of the region passed to the **Franks**, a Germanic tribe, in 788 CE. The Franks emerged as the most powerful rulers in the region. Charlemagne, a Frank and the greatest ruler of the era, developed an empire that extended not only over Slovene lands, but over Germany, France, and much of central Italy. Civil wars followed Charlemagne's death, and his sons divided their father's empire into three kingdoms.

THE HOLY ROMAN EMPIRE

Eventually, the Frank dynasty died out in Germany and gave way to the Saxons. Many historians credit Otto I, a strong Saxon emperor, with founding the Holy Roman Empire in 962 CE. The Holy Roman Empire was a group of territories that stood united by a common faith in Roman Catholicism. While there was one supreme emperor, each territory had its own individual ruler. Constant struggles between these rulers and the empire marked the period. The crown and the Roman Catholic Church also competed for power and influence.

In the early stages of the empire, the emperors were very powerful. As time passed, however, they were forced to grant more and more power to

DATING SYSTEMS AND THEIR MEANING

You might be accustomed to seeing dates expressed with the abbreviations BC or AD, as in the year 1000 BC or the year AD 1900. For centuries, this dating system has been the most common in the Western world. However, since BC and AD are based on Christianity (BC stands for Before Christ and AD stands for *anno Domini*, Latin for "in the year of our Lord"), many people now prefer to use abbreviations that people from all religions can be comfortable using. The abbreviations BCE (meaning Before Common Era) and CE (meaning Common Era) mark time in the same way (for example, 1000 BC is the same year as 1000 BCE, and AD 1900 is the same year as 1900 CE), but BCE and CE do not have the same religious overtones as BC and AD.

regional rulers. The **feudal system** became stronger. The **nobility**, a new class that challenged the emperor, emerged.

At its peak, the empire contained most of the territory that makes up today's Germany, Austria, Slovenia, Switzerland, Belgium, the Netherlands, Luxembourg, Czech Republic, eastern France, northern Italy, and western Poland. Over time, different regions broke away. Under feudal rule, control of Slovenia was passed to the dukes of Bavaria, and at this time the lands were known as the regions of Carinthis, Carniola, and Styria. In 1335, rule of these provinces came under the rule of the Hapsburg family of Austria. They would reign, largely unchallenged until 1918, with the exception of a brief interruption in the early nineteenth century.

HAPSBURG RULE

The Austrian Empire of the Hapsburg family was a major political force in Europe. For six centuries, this family controlled a large area of central Europe and exerted control through measures designed to impose German language and culture on the regions under their rule. As the Hapsburgs developed a large **bureaucracy** to centralize control of education and commerce, German became the primary language of the region, and the Roman Catholic Church controlled the schools.

Over time, the upper classes became completely Germanized. However, the peasant classes were able to maintain the Slovene language

An original bridge of 1842 was augmented in 1931 with two adjacent structures, creating the famous "Triple Bridge" over the Ljubljanica River.

and cultural practices, and as a result, the Slovene people of today retain a strong ethnic identity.

The Age of Enlightenment and Napoleon Bonaparte

By the mid-eighteenth century, during a period known as the Age of Enlightenment, Europe saw remarkable cultural changes characterized by a loss of faith in traditional religious sources of authority and a turn toward human rights, science, and rational thought. Hapsburg rulers Maria Theresa and her son Joseph II instituted reforms based on Enlightenment principles to promote social and economic progress.

The consequences of Enlightenment reforms had widespread significance. The power and authority of the Catholic Church were reduced, and some freedom of worship was established, although the population remained overwhelmingly Roman Catholic. Catholic control of public education was lessened, and the focus of study shifted from theology to the sciences.

By 1809, the French general Napoleon Bonaparte had conquered much of Europe and occupied Slovene lands, in hope of denying the Hapsburgs access to the Adriatic. Now called the Illyrian Provinces, Napoleon established rule over Slovenia, Dalmatia, and part of Croatia; the city of Ljubljana was named provincial capital. French law, based on the **Napoleonic Code**, was instituted. Although the Hapsburgs returned to power by 1814, many of the Napoleonic

reforms in education, law, and public administration remained in place. Thus, Hapsburg rule in Slovenia was slightly less **authoritarian** than in other regions like Bohemia.

The nineteenth century marked a period of national awakening across Central Europe. Napoleon's aggression had created a wave of nationalism. The concept of a nation as a group of people linked by a common language and culture had great appeal to the many different Slavic peoples who had lived for centuries under various forms of foreign rule. Inspired by the renewed interest in German national identity that was taking place among their neighbors, the Slovene intellectual **elite** soon began seeking to proclaim their own nationalist spirit.

Initial national movements were limited to discussions of language, literature, and culture. It was at this time that the Slovene language was first **codified**. Nationalist feeling soon expanded beyond scholarly pursuits, and Slavic nationalists began to form political alliances as well.

By 1848, the Hapsburgs were seeing a series of nationalist demonstrations and revolts across their lands. In 1859, they were driven out of Italy, and by 1866, they were defeated by Germany and expelled from the German Confederation. To strengthen his political power base, Hapsburg emperor Franz Joseph reached out to the Hungarian nobility, and in 1867, he created the Austro-Hungarian Empire.

Slovenia was considered a province of Austria, but because of the great extent to which the Slovene people had been Germanized, they had little conflict with the empire. Austria and Hungary were now united by a common ruler but were otherwise independent states, each with a separate **parliament** and judicial system. Political power rested with ethnic Germans in Austria and Hungarians in Hungary. The empire controlled Czech and Slovak lands as well, and there was more political unrest among the Czech

The Dragon Bridge in Ljubljana was built in 1901, replacing the Butcher's Bridge. The Dragon Bridge was Slovenia's first bridge with asphalt pavement.

Northern Slovenia's climate is dominated by the Alps, with cool moist winds blowing down from the mountains.

and Slovak populations. This was due to their greater numbers, and because they were seen as ethnically more separate from their rulers than the heavily Germanized Slovenes. Slovenian nationalists sought greater Slovenian **autonomy** within the empire, rather than an independent state.

WORLD WAR I
AND THE KINGDOM OF YUGOSLAVIA

The inability of the Austro-Hungarian Empire to ease tensions between the different nationalities under their rule eventually led to the fall of the empire. World War I began on June 28, 1914, when Gavrilo Princip, a Serbian nationalist, assassinated Austrian archduke Franz Ferdinand and his wife, Sophie. Russia allied with Serbia. Germany sided with Austria and soon declared war on Russia. After France declared its support for Russia, Germany attacked France. German troops invaded Belgium, a **neutral** country that stood between German forces and Paris. Great Britain then declared war on Germany.

At the close of World War I, Slovenia was liberated from Austrian rule; in 1918, Slovenia came together with Serbs and Croats to form the "National Council," out of which the Kingdom of Serbs, Croats, and Slovenes was formed under the rule of the king of Serbia. In 1929, the country was renamed the Kingdom of Yugoslavia.

WORLD WAR II
AND THE RISE OF COMMUNISM

By 1933, Adolph Hitler had come to power in nearby Germany, and by 1938, he had occupied neighboring Austria as well. His stated objective was to unify all ethnic German peoples. He soon demanded the surrender of Czechoslovakia's Sudetenland, a disputed region bordering Germany. On September 29, 1938, France, Germany, Italy, and Great Britain signed the Munich Agreement, demanding that Czechoslovakia surrender the Sudetenland to Germany in exchange for a promise of peace. In March 1939, however, Hitler **reneged** on his agreement and invaded the remainder of Czechoslovakia. Nazi aggression continued, and a series of treaties and alliances were invoked as countries sought to defend themselves from the Nazi onslaught. Once again, the world was at war.

Nazi Germany **annexed** most of Slovenia, and over the course of the war the territory was occupied by German, Italian, and Hungarian troops. During the war, most Slovenian resistance activity was organized and carried out by Slovenian **communists**. As the war drew to a close, communism exerted even greater influence in Eastern and Central Europe, strengthened by the presence of victorious Soviet troops in many countries. As different countries and political interests

Many Slovenes favor the bicycle as their mode of transport, especially in the cities.

scrambled for control of the region, Josip Broz Tito established the Socialist Federal Republic of Yugoslavia, of which Slovenia was now a member state. (Tito was born Josip Broz. He adopted the pseudonym Tito in the late 1930s to use in his underground party work.) The country would remain a communist dictatorship until Tito's death in 1980. He was succeeded by a collective presidency.

INDEPENDENCE

By 1989, nationalist sentiments were running high across Yugoslavia. As Serbians and Albanians feuded over Kosovo and began to demand separation from the Yugoslav union, Slovenes also began to demonstrate for a separate state. The Slovenian parliament declared Slovenia's right to **secede** from Yugoslavia in 1989, and in 1991, it declared itself independent as the Republic of Slovenia. A nearly bloodless ten-day war followed, but when greater Yugoslavia saw the Slovene resolve, they withdrew their forces peacefully. As its neighbors warred over territory and ethnic differences, Slovenia begins to implement anti-communist reforms and becomes a stable democratic republic.

The Slovenia of today is one of the most prosperous of the former communist states in central Europe, and it has one of the strongest economies in the region. In 2004, Slovenia became a member of NATO and the EU and is one of the fastest growing tourist destinations in Europe. The tourist industry is helping the Slovene economy grow even more.

The steps of the Franciscan church in the old town of Ljubljana are a favored spot for musicians, young people, and anyone who wants to watch the city's nightlife.

3 THE ECONOMY

Although Slovenia is still in recovery from the economic blight that marked its years under communist rule, it is by far the most economically developed of the former Yugoslav states. Once considered to be the "Switzerland of Yugoslavia," Slovenia had enjoyed a greater degree of economic freedom than the other Yugoslavian states of Serbia, Croatia, and Bosnia. This has enabled the new nation to make great strides in increasing its economic power.

QUICK FACTS: THE ECONOMY OF SLOVENIA

Gross Domestic Product (GDP): US$36.82 billion

GDP per capita: $US19,000

Industries: ferrous metallurgy and aluminum products, lead and zinc smelting, electronics, trucks, electric power equipment, wood products, textiles, chemicals, machine tools

Agriculture: potatoes, hops, wheat, sugar beets, corn grapes; cattle, sheep, poultry

Export commodities: manufactured goods, machinery and transport equipment, chemicals, food

Export partners: Germany 23.2%, Italy 13.2%, Croatia 9%, Austria 7.3%, France 5.7%, Bosnia and Herzegovina 4.2% (2003)

Import commodities: machinery and transport equipment, manufactured goods, chemicals, fuels and lubricants, food

Import partners: Germany 19.3%, Italy 18.3%, France 10%, Austria 8.6% (2003)

Currency: tolar (SIT)

Currency exchange rate: US$1 = 182.60 SIT (December 20, 2004)

Note: All figures are from 2004 unless otherwise noted.
Source: www.cia.gov, 2005.

AN ECONOMY IN TRANSITION

Slovenia's rapid economic recovery can be linked directly to the many advantages it enjoys over the region's other emerging economies. Because of their traditional ties with Western Europe, the Slovenes were able to effectively market the many economic possibilities of a free and independent Slovenia to foreign investors. A dramatic increase in trade, especially in the manufacturing and tourism sectors, has been their reward.

Unlike many of the **Eastern Bloc** countries, Yugoslavia permitted a degree of private ownership in Slovenia. Under the communist system, a giant bureaucracy was required to maintain absolute governmental ownership and control of industry. As a result, a large portion of workers in these countries were employed in administrative jobs. As industries in these countries made the shift to private ownership, these large bureaucracies became unnecessary, leaving a high number of unemployed workers with no competitive skills. By comparison, more than 60 percent of the Slovene workforce was employed directly in production. As a result, Slovenia today boasts low unemployment and a highly skilled and productive workforce.

During its years under the government of Yugoslavia, Slovenia produced 30 percent of all Yugoslav goods for foreign export. This is extraordinary, given that Slovenia made up only 8 percent of the total population. Foreign investors today see

Ljubljana has modern supermarkets, but many still favor the city's open-air market by the river.

Slovenes are enjoying the variety of choices in merchandise that the free market system has brought them.

this historical productivity as one of many advantages to investing in Slovenia. As Slovenia is ethnically **homogeneous**, it has avoided the wars that have plagued the other Yugoslav states of Croatia, Serbia, and Bosnia. The political situation is stable and democratic, and important reforms have been made to create a hospitable business environment. Investment and economic growth since achieving independence has been rapid.

MANUFACTURING AND TOURISM: THE MAINSTAYS OF THE ECONOMY

Slovenia is the most industrialized of all the former Yugoslav republics. Economic growth in all sectors has been on the rise since the country achieved its independence in 1991. Manufacturing remains the heart of Slovenian enterprise.

Iron, steel, aluminum, heavy machinery, motor vehicles, cement, chemicals, and leather are the main industries of the region. Light engineering and electronics are also some new areas of enterprise. Transition from government to private ownership of industry was quick and efficient, and many new laws have been passed to assure that conditions in Slovenia are favorable to business. The traditional trade relationships between Slovenia and large European markets like Germany go back to the days of Hapsburg rule, and have enabled Slovenian products to maintain a foothold in the marketplace at a time when products made in the Eastern Bloc nations have often had a negative reputation.

Tourism has also grown tremendously since Slovenia's independence. With EU membership easing travel between member nations, Slovenia has seen a large increase in the number of European tourists who enjoy combining aspects of Alpine and Mediterranean vacations in the same trip for a minimal expense. Slovenia was recently voted the favorite European travel destination by readers of a major British travel magazine. The Slovenian government has targeted the tourism industry as one that is ready to explode and has stepped up marketing efforts to lure **ecotourists** looking for an "unspoiled" corner of Europe.

AGRICULTURE

Small private farms prevail in Slovenia, although it also has a number of agricultural companies. A large proportion of citizens live in the countryside. However, relatively few are active in agriculture as a business due to the small size of individual land holdings. As a result, Slovene farms are mostly of a mixed type, growing small crops of many different items for private use.

The influence of the Mediterranean and continental climates allows the cultivation of various fruits and the production of wine. In addition to producing food and wood, agriculture has an important role in traditional Slovene culture. Conditions in the Alpine regions are well suited to grazing, and cattle raising in the mountains is common. These areas produce more than half of all the country's milk and meat.

ENERGY

Lignite and coal are the principal domestic sources of energy in Slovenia. Environmental protection and resource **conservation** are important factors of Slovenia's new, EU-driven energy policy, and the Slovene government is investing in research for renewable energy supplies. Slovenia also relies on imported oil and natural gas, as well as on nuclear energy provided by a plant jointly maintained by Croatia.

TRANSPORTATION

Highways, railways, waterways (both navigable rivers and the port city of Koper), and airports make up Slovenia's transportation system. A modern transportation structure enables rapid and easy connections to other European trade centers. Daily flights connect Ljubljana Airport with other international capitals such as London, Moscow, Istanbul, Paris, and Berlin. By 2004, Slovenia spent the equivalent of US$4 billion to modernize its highways, and in the years between 2000 and 2004, the government invested the equivalent of US$460 million in updating the national telecommunications network and available services.

The climate of Slovenia allows cultivation of a variety of foodstuffs.

Despite Slovenia's relatively healthy economy, some are critical of the changes that occurred in the nation.

LOOKING FORWARD

Slovenia has made outstanding accomplishments in privatizing its industries and modernizing the national *infrastructure*. Of all the new members of the EU, little Slovenia has some of the most promising prospects for continued economic growth. Foreign investors have begun to realize the potential for increased economic development.

Like many of its formerly communist neighbors in Central and Eastern Europe, Slovenia is still a country in transition. However, great advances have been made in the last decade, and all indicators are that this tiny nation may become a powerhouse of economic growth.

The artistic talents of the Slovenes are visible in museums and on the walls of the capital city Ljubljana.

4 SLOVENIA'S PEOPLE AND CULTURE

CHAPTER

With a population of just two million people, Slovenia is one of the smallest countries in Europe, with a total area smaller than that of New Jersey. Throughout history, the Slovene people have been ruled by foreign powers. The fact that their culture not only survives today, but thrives, is a testament to their strong instincts about the preservation of their heritage.

Quick Facts: The People of Slovenia

Population: 2,011,473 (July 2004 est.)

Ethnic groups: Slovene 92%, Croat 1%, Serb 0.5%, Hungarian 0.4%, Bosniak 0.3%, other 5.8% (1991)

Age structure:
- *0-14* years: 14.3%
- *15-64* years: 70.6%
- *65 years and over:* 15.1%

Population growth rate: -0.01%

Birth rate: 8.9 births/1,000 pop.

Death rate: 10.15 deaths/1,000 pop.

Migration rate: 1,12 migrant(s)/1,000 pop.

Infant mortality rate: 4.5 deaths/1,000 live births

Life expectancy at birth:
- *Total population:* 75.93
- *Male:* 72.18
- *Female:* 79.92

Total fertility rate: 1.23 children born/woman

Religions: Roman Catholic (Uniate 2%) 70.8%, Lutheran 1%, Muslim 1%, atheist 4.3%

Languages: Slovenian 92%, Serbo-Coratian 6.2%, other 1.8%

Literacy rate: 99.7% (2003 est.)

Note: All figures are from 2004 unless otherwise noted.
Source: www.cia.gov, 2005.

Slovenia is ethnically homogeneous, as almost 90 percent of the people are ethnic Slovenes. The remaining populace is a mixture of Hungarians and Italians in the border regions, and a very small number of ethnic minorities from the other former Yugoslav states. Most of these relocated to Slovenia for economic reasons and have since obtained Slovene citizenship. The rights of minorities are clearly protected under the constitution.

Religion: Strongly Roman Catholic

Slovene culture is very closely tied to the Roman Catholic Church. More than 70 percent of Slovenes today remain Roman Catholic, even after years of institutionalized atheism while under communist rule. Slovenes identified so strongly with the Catholic religion that most people continued to worship openly and observe religious holidays in defiance of laws banning such practices.

Food and Drink: A Crossroads for Cuisine

Slovene cuisine has been heavily influenced by the country's location between the Alps of Austria and Italy. As a result, traditional favorites have been adopted both from the heartier German-inspired dishes of the north as well as Mediterranean fare

The capital of Ljubljana has a thriving café culture, where tourists and residents enjoy the mild evenings by eating and drinking into the night.

from the south. Slovene menus offer a mix of dishes such as **strudels**, sausages, sauerkraut, potato salad, beef and venison prepared in mushroom sauce, as well as pizza and **polenta**. Other foods include Balkan treats such as smoked hams and hard salamis. Potica (pronounced paw-TEE-zah) is a traditional Slovene dessert bread that can be purchased in bakeries throughout the country, and consists of flaky pastry surrounding a sweet nut filling.

Like its neighbors in the region, Slovenia is sprinkled with small vineyards. The traditional Slovene wine, Dolenjiski Cvicek, is a very dry, red wine produced in the southeast area of the coun-

Music is an important part of the Slovene culture. A capella singers in this Ljubljana café meet to harmonize weekly.

try. Other vineyards produce sweeter white wines, and a host of fruit-flavored liqueurs are produced in Slovenia as well.

The latest trend in Slovenian dining is known as the "slow food movement." A slow food meal takes place in a private home among family and close friends. This type of meal consists of eight or more courses, eaten over a period of hours. The menu focuses on locally grown produce and old family recipes, and a new wine is introduced to accompany each course.

EDUCATION: A SYSTEM IN TRANSITION

At present, the educational system in Slovenia is undergoing a series of changes and reforms. These changes are aimed at promoting academic excellence in Slovenia and evening the playing field between students educated in tiny Slovenia and students educated in the larger, wealthier nations of Western Europe.

In 1999, compulsory education lasting for nine years began to be implemented. The first six years, designed for students age six to twelve, provide a basic elementary education. The last three years are very similar to American high school, with students studying a specialized program of individual subjects. At the end of nine years, the student is considered to have completed basic education.

Secondary education is then selected from a two- to three-year program of vocational study or, for students who wish to pursue university studies, a four-year technical program. The secondary education technical program requires a student to pass a comprehensive final exam, called the *policna matura*, which qualifies the student for university entrance.

FESTIVALS AND EVENTS: A PROUD CULTURAL HERITAGE

The Slovenes have many festivals that celebrate their rich cultural heritage. There is a strong feeling in Slovenia that the traditions of the past must be observed even in the midst of busy modern life. Major religious holidays such as Christmas and Easter center not only on religious worship but also on traditional Slovene foods and decorations.

The tiny nation also hosts thousands of cultural events featuring the performing or visual arts. Small towns have ethnic festivals featuring traditional dress, folk music, and dancing. The larger cities and tourist areas have numerous art galleries and exhibits, stage performances of every conceivable type, and concerts ranging from classical music and Slovene folk music, to western pop and hip hop. One of the most popular annual events in Ljubljana is the Jazz Festival.

Singers and instrumentalists evangelize through song in front of a church in downtown Ljubljana.

SPORTS

Slovene lands have been the home to a variety of sports dating back to Roman times. Later writings tell of Slovenes pursuing boating, hunting, fishing, mountaineering, and shooting. In 1689, the oldest recorded description of skiing was noted in Slovenia.

Modern Slovenes pursue many of the same types of sport, having cheered medal-winning Olympic performances in many alpine events, rowing, and gymnastics. The annual Ski-Jumping World Cup takes place in Slovenia each year, and Slovene Davo Karnicar became the first person to ever ski nonstop from the summit of Mount Everest to its base. Jolanda Ceplak is the reigning European champion in the indoor and outdoor 800-meter run.

LANGUAGE AND LITERATURE: A FOUNDATION FOR NATIONAL IDENTITY

The first books written in Slovene date back to the sixteenth century, and were mainly religious texts. It was the Slovene poet France Preseren who established through his works the greatest national awareness of the Slovene language. Today, the national award for culture bears his name.

Throughout history, the Slovene language has played a critical role in preserving other aspects of Slovene heritage. Despite centuries of influence from foreign powers, the Slovenes have managed to preserve the distinct linguistic features of their language and pass that down through the generations. This ability to maintain their language despite constant occupation is a source of national pride.

The slow Ljubljanica River winds through the capital of Slovenia, curving around the foot of Castle Hill.

5 THE CITIES

Population in Slovenia tends to be centered around small villages and cities. These urban centers provide valuable opportunities for education and employment yet are small and easily navigated by visitors. The region is filled with telltale signs of the land's varied history. Depending on what part of the country you are in, you may see ornate examples of Venetian-inspired architecture, Roman ruins, historic cathedrals, churches, and bridges, or a modern city high rise. Like the landscape, the cities of Slovenia offer great diversity in a limited area.

LJUBLJANA:
THE CAPITAL

Ljubljana is Slovenia's capital and most-populated city. It has stood for almost 5,000 years and has retained traces from all of the many periods of its history. Considered a medium-sized European city, Ljubljana preserves a small-town atmosphere while serving as the nation's political, cultural, and economic center.

Ljubljana has always been a cultural and educational hub. Today the city hosts 500,000 students, many studying from foreign countries; all bring with them their own special contributions to the city's atmosphere. More than 10,000 different cultural events and festivals take place here each year, including ten international festivals. Its geographic position in the very heart of Europe has earned it a reputation as an important meeting place for leaders and merchants. The treaty that ended the Napoleonic Wars was negotiated in this peaceful city, and today rail and air transport can take you to almost any corner of Europe in a matter of hours.

PIRAN:
A PARADISE ON THE ADRIATIC

Piran is the most frequently visited tourist destination in Slovenia. Located on the Adriatic coast, this city has a history reaching far back to the days of ancient Rome. Mediterranean in feel, Piran is home to numerous vineyards and olive groves. Many local wines and high-quality olive oils are produced here, although the main economic activity in the city today is tourism.

Visitors to Piran can enjoy a wide variety of activities. The city features numerous hotels, beaches, restaurants, nightclubs, and a large casino in addition to its historical attractions and beaches. Retreats and spas are available to assist weary travelers escape the hectic pace of modern life, and many venues exist to occupy the nature enthusiast.

BLED:
AN ALPINE RETREAT

Nestled high in the Alps alongside a spectacular glacial lake, Bled typifies the character of northern Slovenia, much as Piran does the south. Essentially a medieval city, Bled was once the seat of the Catholic bishop, and the castle they left behind was later the favorite summer home of the Yugoslav royal family. Perched high atop a steep cliff, the castle provides some of the best mountain views in Central Europe.

The area abounds in year-round recreational activities—from alpine sports to bird watching and fishing. Swimming and rowing are common pastimes in the summer months, and the lake freezes

At night, Ljubljana is alive with lights and life.
Not surprisingly, the city has been the home of celebrated national poets and artists.

in winter, allowing ice-skating. Winter visitors sometimes use skates to reach destinations on other parts of the lake.

Many picturesque inns and taverns are situated all around the lake, which was created 14,000 years ago when a glacier slid into the valley. A tiny island remains in the center of the lake, home to historic St. Mary's Church. Legend has it that anyone who climbs the ninety-nine stairs to the top of the belfry to ring the wishing bell will have his wish come true.

This graffiti vision of an urban landscape painted on a city wall seems far from Ljubljana's charming and slow feeling.

Koper:
The Port City

Koper, just thirteen miles (21 kilometers) south of Trieste, Italy, is a unique blend of historical treasures and modern industrial sites. Once the capital of Istria under the Venetian Republic, the city still retains a medieval Italian feeling. In contrast to its marble facades and ornate squares, Koper also features the container ports, highways, railways, and warehouses of a major port city. Koper is a critical port not only for Slovenia, but for Austria and many other neighboring states as well.

Slovenia's cities are small and less well known than other more famous European cities, but these hubs of tourism and industry have helped make Slovenia a valuable member of the EU.

The EU flag

6

THE FORMATION OF THE EUROPEAN UNION

The EU is an economic and political confederation of twenty-five European nations. Member countries abide by common foreign and security policies and cooperate on judicial and domestic affairs. The confederation, however, does not replace existing states or governments. Each of the twenty-five member states is *autonomous*, but they have all agreed to establish some common institutions and to hand over some of their own decision-making powers to these international bodies. As a result, decisions on matters that interest all member states can be made democratically, accommodating everyone's concerns and interests.

Today, the EU is the most powerful regional organization in the world. It has evolved from a primarily economic organization to an increasingly political one. Besides promoting economic cooperation, the EU requires that its members uphold fundamental values of peace and **solidarity**, human dignity, freedom, and equality. Based on the principles of democracy and the rule of law, the EU respects the culture and organizations of member states.

HISTORY

The seeds of the EU were planted more than fifty years ago in a Europe reduced to smoking piles of rubble by two world wars. European nations suffered great financial difficulties in the postwar period. They were struggling to get back on their feet and realized that another war would cause further hardship. Knowing that internal conflict was hurting all of Europe, a drive began toward European cooperation.

France took the first historic step. On May 9, 1950 (now celebrated as Europe Day), Robert Schuman, the French foreign minister, proposed the coal and steel industries of France and West Germany be coordinated under a single supranational authority. The proposal, known as the Treaty

of Paris, attracted four other countries—Belgium, Luxembourg, the Netherlands, and Italy—and resulted in the 1951 formation of the European Coal and Steel Community (ECSC). These six countries became the founding members of the EU.

In 1957, European cooperation took its next big leap. Under the Treaty of Rome, the European Economic Community (EEC) and the European Atomic Energy Community (EURATOM) were formed. Informally known as the Common Market, the EEC promoted joining the national economies into a single European economy. The 1965 Treaty of Brussels (more commonly referred to as the Merger Treaty) united these various treaty organizations under a single umbrella, the European Community (EC).

In 1992, the Maastricht Treaty (also known as the Treaty of the European Union) was signed in Maastricht, the Netherlands, signaling the birth of the EU as it stands today. **Ratified** the following year, the Maastricht Treaty provided for a central banking system, a common currency (the euro) to replace the national currencies, a legal definition of the EU, and a framework for expanding the

The EU's united economy has allowed it to become a worldwide financial power.

EU's political role, particularly in the area of foreign and security policy.

By 1993, the member countries completed their move toward a single market and agreed to participate in a larger common market, the European Economic Area, established in 1994.

The EU, headquartered in Brussels, Belgium, reached its current member strength in spurts. In

The euro, the EU's currency

1973, Denmark, Ireland, and the United Kingdom joined the six founding members of the EC. They were followed by Greece in 1981, and Portugal and Spain in 1986. The 1990s saw the unification of the two Germanys, and as a result, East Germany entered the EU fold. Austria, Finland, and Sweden joined the EU in 1995, bringing the total number of member states to fifteen. In 2004, the EU nearly doubled its size when ten countries—Cyprus, the Czech Republic, Estonia, Hungary, Latvia, Lithuania, Malta, Poland, Slovakia, and Slovenia—became members.

THE EU FRAMEWORK

The EU's structure has often been compared to a "roof of a temple with three columns." As established by the Maastricht Treaty, this three-pillar framework encompasses all the policy areas—or pillars—of European cooperation. The three pillars of the EU are the European Community, the Common Foreign and Security Policy (CFSP), and Police and Judicial Co-operation in Criminal Matters.

QUICK FACTS: THE EUROPEAN UNION

Number of Member Countries: 25
Official Languages: 20—Czech, Danish, Dutch, English, Estonian, Finnish, French, German, Greek, Hungarian, Italian, Latvian, Lithuanian, Maltese, Polish, Portuguese, Slovak, Slovenian, Spanish, and Swedish; additional language for treaty purposes: Irish Gaelic
Motto: *In Varietate Concordia* (United in Diversity)
European Council's President: Each member state takes a turn to lead the council's activities for 6 months.
European Commission's President: José Manuel Barroso (Portugal)
European Parliament's President: Josep Borrell (Spain)
Total Area: 1,502,966 square miles (3,892,685 sq. km.)
Population: 454,900,000
Population Density: 302.7 people/square mile (116.8 people/sq. km.)
GDP: €9.61.1012
Per Capita GDP: €21,125
Formation:
- Declared: February 7, 1992, with signing of the Maastricht Treaty
- Recognized: November 1, 1993, with the ratification of the Maastricht Treaty

Community Currency: Euro. Currently 12 of the 25 member states have adopted the euro as their currency.
Anthem: "Ode to Joy"
Flag: Blue background with 12 gold stars arranged in a circle
Official Day: Europe Day, May 9

Source: europa.eu.int

PILLAR ONE

The European Community pillar deals with economic, social, and environmental policies. It is a body consisting of the European Parliament, European Commission, European Court of Justice, Council of the European Union, and the European Courts of Auditors.

PILLAR TWO

The idea that the EU should speak with one voice in world affairs is as old as the European integration process itself. Toward this end, the Common Foreign and Security Policy (CFSP) was formed in 1993.

PILLAR THREE

The cooperation of EU member states in judicial and criminal matters ensures that its citizens enjoy the freedom to travel, work, and live securely and safely anywhere within the EU. The third pillar— Police and Judicial Co-operation in Criminal Matters—helps to protect EU citizens from international crime and to ensure equal access to justice and fundamental rights across the EU.

The flags of the EU's nations:

top row, left to right
Belgium, the Czech Republic, Denmark, Germany, Estonia, Greece

second row, left to right
Spain, France, Ireland, Italy, Cyprus, Latvia

third row, left to right
Lithuania, Luxembourg, Hungary, Malta, the Netherlands, Austria

bottom row, left to right
Poland, Portugal, Slovenia, Slovakia, Finland, Sweden, United Kingdom

ECONOMIC STATUS

As of May 2004, the EU had the largest economy in the world, followed closely by the United States. But even though the EU continues to enjoy a trade surplus, it faces the twin problems of high unemployment rates and **stagnancy**.

The 2004 addition of ten new member states is expected to boost economic growth. EU membership is likely to stimulate the economies of these relatively poor countries. In turn, their prosperity growth will be beneficial to the EU.

THE EURO

The EU's official currency is the euro, which came into circulation on January 1, 2002. The shift to the euro has been the largest monetary changeover in the world. Twelve countries— Belgium, Germany, Greece, Spain, France, Ireland, Italy, Luxembourg, the Netherlands, Finland, Portugal, and Austria—have adopted it as their currency.

SINGLE MARKET

Within the EU, laws of member states are harmonized and domestic policies are coordinated to create a larger, more-efficient single market.

The chief features of the EU's internal policy on the single market are:

- free trade of goods and services

- a common EU competition law that controls anticompetitive activities of companies and member states

- removal of internal border control and harmonization of external controls between member states

- freedom for citizens to live and work anywhere in the EU as long as they are not dependent on the state

- free movement of **capital** between member states

- harmonization of government regulations, corporation law, and trademark registration

- a single currency

- coordination of environmental policy

- a common agricultural policy and a common fisheries policy

- a common system of indirect taxation, the value-added tax (VAT), and common customs duties and **excise**

- funding for research

- funding for aid to disadvantaged regions

The EU's external policy on the single market specifies:

- a common external **tariff** and a common position in international trade negotiations

- funding of programs in other Eastern European countries and developing countries

COOPERATION AREAS

EU member states cooperate in other areas as well. Member states can vote in European Parliament elections. Intelligence sharing and cooperation in criminal matters are carried out through EUROPOL and the Schengen Information System.

The EU is working to develop common foreign and security policies. Many member states are resisting such a move, however, saying these are sensitive areas best left to individual member states. Arguing in favor of a common approach to security and foreign policy are countries like France and Germany, who insist that a safer and more secure Europe can only become a reality under the EU umbrella.

One of the EU's great achievements has been to create a boundary-free area within which people, goods, services, and money can move around freely; this ease of movement is sometimes called "the four freedoms." As the EU grows in size, so do the challenges facing it—and yet its fifty-year history has amply demonstrated the power of cooperation.

Europe is proud of its "bright idea," a union with economic and political power.

The EU believes that it can use its power to act as a "lighthouse" for the rest of the world.

KEY EU INSTITUTIONS

Five key institutions play a specific role in the EU.

THE EUROPEAN PARLIAMENT

The European Parliament (EP) is the democratic voice of the people of Europe. Directly elected every five years, the Members of the European Parliament (MEPs) sit not in national **blocs** but in political groups representing the seven main political parties of the member states. Each group reflects the political ideology of the national parties to which its members belong. Some MEPs are not attached to any political group.

COUNCIL OF THE EUROPEAN UNION

The Council of the European Union (formerly known as the Council of Ministers) is the main leg-

EUROPEAN UNION—SLOVENIA

islative and decision-making body in the EU. It brings together the nationally elected representatives of the member-state governments. One minister from each of the EU's member states attends council meetings. It is the forum in which government representatives can assert their interests and reach compromises. Increasingly, the Council of the European Union and the EP are acting together as colegislators in decision-making processes.

EUROPEAN COMMISSION

The European Commission does much of the day-to-day work of the EU. Politically independent, the commission represents the interests of the EU as a whole, rather than those of individual member states. It drafts proposals for new European laws, which it presents to the EP and the Council of the European Union. The European Commission makes sure EU decisions are implemented properly and supervises the way EU funds are spent. It also sees that everyone abides by the European treaties and European law.

The EU member-state governments choose the European Commission president, who is then approved by the EP. Member states, in consultation with the incoming president, nominate the other European Commission members, who must also be approved by the EP. The commission is appointed for a five-year term, but can be dismissed by the EP. Many members of its staff work in Brussels, Belgium.

COURT OF JUSTICE

Headquartered in Luxembourg, the Court of Justice of the European Communities consists of one independent judge from each EU country. This court ensures that the common rules decided in the EU are understood and followed uniformly by all the members. The Court of Justice settles disputes over how EU treaties and legislation are interpreted. If national courts are in doubt about how to apply EU rules, they must ask the Court of Justice. Individuals can also bring proceedings against EU institutions before the court.

COURT OF AUDITORS

EU funds must be used legally, economically, and for their intended purpose. The Court of Auditors, an independent EU institution located in Luxembourg, is responsible for overseeing how EU money is spent. In effect, these auditors help European taxpayers get better value for the money that has been channeled into the EU.

OTHER IMPORTANT BODIES

1. European Economic and Social Committee: expresses the opinions of organized civil society on economic and social issues

2. Committee of the Regions: expresses the opinions of regional and local authorities

3. European Central Bank: responsible for monetary policy and managing the euro

4. European Ombudsman: deals with citizens' complaints about mismanagement by any EU institution or body

5. European Investment Bank: helps achieve EU objectives by financing investment projects

Together with a number of agencies and other bodies completing the system, the EU's institutions have made it the most powerful organization in the world.

EU Member States

In order to become a member of the EU, a country must have a stable democracy that guarantees the rule of law, human rights, and protection of minorities. It must also have a functioning market economy as well as a civil service capable of applying and managing EU laws.

The EU provides substantial financial assistance and advice to help candidate countries prepare themselves for membership. As of October 2004, the EU has twenty-five member states. Bulgaria and Romania are likely to join in 2007, which would bring the EU's total population to nearly 500 million.

In December 2004, the EU decided to open negotiations with Turkey on its proposed membership. Turkey's possible entry into the EU has been fraught with controversy. Much of this controversy has centered on Turkey's human rights record and the divided island of Cyprus. If allowed to join the EU, Turkey would be its most-populous member state.

The 2004 expansion was the EU's most ambitious enlargement to date. Never before has the EU embraced so many new countries, grown so much in terms of area and population, or encompassed so many different histories and cultures. As the EU moves forward into the twenty-first century, it will undoubtedly continue to grow in both political and economic strength.

The capital of Slovenia has managed to maintain an old-style charm, while opening itself to modern commercial enterprises.

CHAPTER 7
SLOVENIA IN THE EUROPEAN UNION

Ten new member nations were admitted to the European Union in 2004. These nations were Slovenia, Cyprus, Estonia, Hungary, Latvia, Lithuania, Malta, Poland, the Czech Republic, and Slovakia. Eight of these ten states, including Slovenia, were formerly communist nations, and all are making important adjustments in order to become more politically and economically attuned with the established EU states. Slovenia has the advantage of being one of the most stable and prosperous of the new member states.

A More Prominent Role on the World Stage

As one of the smallest nations in Europe, and a nation that is culturally **insular**, Slovenia for many years has neglected its public profile. In many parts of the world, people confuse Slovenia with the larger country of Slovakia, or mistakenly assume that Slovenia is embroiled in the ethnic conflicts that have plagued the other former Yugoslav states. As a new member of both the EU and NATO, Slovenia is working hard to raise awareness of its nation and the many benefits to investing in Slovenia.

Differing Views of a United Europe

Public opinion in Europe remains divided about the amount of decision-making control member nations should surrender to the EU. Many smaller EU nations, along with certain major European powers such as Great Britain, favor surrendering a minimum level of **sovereignty**, especially over such things as defense and foreign policy. Concern has been expressed that as a nation who has only recently gained a democratically elected legislative body, the Slovene voting public should have more control over legislation being passed than the European Parliament in Brussels. Slovenes

EUROPEAN UNION—SLOVENIA

A wide range of architectural styles are visible within Ljubljana, from Baroque to the Art-Nouveau.

feel that there is a critical need to ensure that their national identity is not weakened by giving up too much control to a centralized EU government. Currently Slovenia and most of the other new EU states support a policy termed intergovernmentalism—a governmental approach in which member states must decide on policy by unanimous agreement. Slovaks remain concerned that their status as a new member of the EU, and their relative economic weakness, puts their interests behind those of larger countries like Germany in EU decision making.

Other, primarily larger EU countries feel strongly that the greatest opportunities for growth can be found within the framework of a strongly united Europe. Supporters of supranationalism—a governmental approach in which EU member states would bound by decisions based on majority rule—believe that the benefits of having common policies for defense, treaty negotiation, and trade far outweigh the individual interests of separate member states. Time will tell which approach eventually wins out, and what the impact will be on smaller nations like Slovenia.

SLOVENIA AS A PARTNER IN TRADE

Being a small nation has unique challenges. In many respects, large countries have tended to ignore Slovenia as a market; after all, many cities have larger populations than this entire country. As an end market for goods, the prospects for expanding trade in the country are not that exciting.

However, where Slovenia has excelled is in marketing itself as a trading partner, assisting firms from other nations establish better trade relationships. For example, where Slovenia once tried to distance itself from the other former Yugoslav states, Slovenia now acts almost as a broker, easing trade between its new EU partners and the Balkan nations, who are still years away from being ready for EU membership themselves. They also work with companies in the former communist states to manufacture products jointly in Slovenia, so that the products benefit from their association with the high quality standards associated with Slovenia. This approach has created exciting growth for the tiny nation.

OPPORTUNITIES AND AREAS OF CONCERN

Slovenia is eager to capitalize on the new benefits of its EU membership. Among these are the millions of dollars available in funds for a variety of projects, designed to enhance the ability of Slovenia to maintain the same standards as the other larger members of the EU. Slovenes enthusiastically threw their support behind EU membership, expecting to have access to these financial resources to further develop the country's infrastructure, as well as to support research that would expand agriculture, develop new energy sources, and help to create new technology.

Unfortunately, this may be one area where Slovenia's relative prosperity could work against it. Currently the standard of living in Slovenia is very

Slovenia has opened up to trade, using its position as a broker to facilitate trading relationships between the EU and other Balkan nations.

Slovenians are attempting to harmonize with European interests as their country manages its new position in the European Union.

close to that enjoyed in the larger nations of the EU. It is the first of the new member states to have moved off the World Bank Recipient List onto the Donor List; Slovenia is now in the position of making loans to other governments and is developing solid reserves of foreign currency. Because of these successes, access to EU development funds could be cut off to Slovenia as early as 2007.

A BRIGHT FUTURE

As Slovenia looks forward to a bright new economic and political future, there are still some areas that need to change if the infant nation is to make the most of its opportunities as a new member of the EU. In the past, Slovenia has made its reforms gradually, which has contributed to the security and stability of the small nation. Now, however, the nation must act quickly to take advantage of the assistance and financial aid of greater Europe. In any case, all indicators are that tiny Slovenia has a bright future ahead.

A Calendar of Slovenian Festivals

Slovenia celebrates many religious, historical, and cultural festivals. The majority of Slovene holidays are affiliated with the Roman Catholic Church, although a list of public holidays follows. All public offices are closed for these holidays, and workers generally get a day off to celebrate and rest.

January: January 1 is a public holiday. The **New Year** festivities traditionally include champagne and fireworks, and are celebrated in Slovenia in a similar fashion to the celebrations that take place across Europe.

February: February 8 is **Preseren Day**, the Slovenian National Cultural holiday. The holiday is named for the Slovene poet France Preseren, who is regarded as having raised respect and awareness for the Slovene language and culture. All public offices are closed and art, music, and cultural festivals of all kinds can be found across the country on this holiday.

March/April: Easter may fall in March or April, and is celebrated for two days on Easter Sunday and Easter Monday. Families in Slovenia celebrate with a special breakfast featuring ham, eggs, horseradish, and the traditional Slovene dessert potica. Easter eggs are also an important part of the celebration, but the look of the eggs varies widely in different parts of the country. Crushed eggshells are thought to bring good luck, and are spread around homes for protection. April 27 is **Uprising Against Occupation Day**, which commemorates the Slovene resistance movement of World War II.

May: Labor Day is celebrated on May 1 and 2. This festival has its roots as a communist holiday where workers would celebrate work. Now, Slovenes celebrate by enjoying some time off and spending leisure time with their families.

June: June 25 is **Statehood Day**, and commemorates the proclamation of Slovenian Independence in 1991.

August/September: The Catholic festival celebrating **Assumption Day** occurs on August 15. This is a recognized public holiday. August and September also are months when many villages have small festivals to celebrate the harvest.

October: October 31 is **Reformation Day**, a celebration of the life of Martin Luther and his Protestant Reformation. Although it may seem a strange holiday to observe in a predominantly Roman Catholic country, Slovenes credit Luther's insistence that the Bible be translated into languages other than Latin with the conversion of the Slovene language into the written word.

November: All Saints' Day on November 1 is an important religious holiday in Slovenia. People use the day off from work to travel to the graves of their ancestors and decorate cemeteries.

December: On December 25, **Christmas** is celebrated as it is across the Christian world. It is always an occasion for families to gather, share a meal, and decorate a tree, but other traditions vary widely from region to region. December 26 is **Independence Day**, celebrated with fireworks and national celebrations.

Krofi (Slovene Doughnuts)

Makes 65 doughnuts

Ingredients
3 packages dry yeast
1 cup milk
1 cup half and half cream
6 tablespoons butter
6 tablespoons margarine
6 large eggs
3/4 cup sugar
1 teaspoon salt
1 cup sour cream
1/2 lemon
3 pounds flour
powdered sugar

Directions
Prepare yeast according to package directions and set aside to rise. Heat milk, cream, butter, and margarine; mix well, then cool to luke-warm. In a large bowl, beat eggs, sugar, salt, and sour cream together. Add to milk mixture. Stir in yeast, grated rind and juice from lemon, and two cups of flour. Beat until smooth. Continue to add remaining flour until dough is easy to handle. Place dough on floured surface and knead about ten minutes. Place dough in a greased bowl, turning to grease all sides. Cover with a towel and allow dough to rise for about two hours. Then, on floured surface, stretch (do not roll) the dough to about a half-inch thickness. Use a glass to cut rounds (there are no holes in krofi) and allow rounds to rise for an additional thirty minutes. Deep-fry rounds in three inches of oil until golden brown on both sides, turning once. Dust with powdered sugar.

Zganci (Corn Mush)

This is a favorite side dish in the alpine regions of Slovenia.

Serves 6

Ingredients
1 cup plus 1 teaspoon of water
1/2 pound corn flour or buckwheat flour
3 tablespoons bacon fat with cracklings
salt to taste

Directions
Boil water and salt. Add flour but do not stir. Allow to boil for five minutes. Take a wooden spoon and poke a hole in the middle of the lump, then continue to boil for ten more minutes. Pour off half the water and let stand until water is absorbed. Then, stir in hot bacon fat and let stand for another five minutes. Top with crumbled bacon pieces.

Krompirjeva Solata (Potato Salad)

The Slovene version of a traditional favorite.

Serves 4–6

Ingredients
6 medium potatoes, peeled and diced
1 onion, sliced thin
4 tablespoons apple cider vinegar
3 tablespoons olive oil
1 teaspoon salt
pepper to taste

Directions
Boil potatoes in skin until cooked. Drain and slice thinly into a large salad bowl. Toss gently with other ingredients and serve.

Slovenian Barley Soup

Ingredients

1 1/2–2 pounds smoked meat (ham, smoked pork chops, pork loin, smoked sausage, or ham bone with meat)
1 1/2 cups medium pearl barley
1 tablespoon salt
1 medium sliced carrot
few sprigs of parsley
1 medium diced potato
1 fresh tomato, quartered
1 medium onion
1 clove garlic

Directions
Wash barley thoroughly and drain. In a large soup pot, place the barley, meat, carrots, potatoes, and salt. In the center of a square of cheesecloth or other clean white cloth, place parsley, garlic, and onion. Gather edges together, and tie securely with clean string.* Add to the soup pot and add 2 quarts of water, adding more if soup becomes too thick during the cooking process. Bring to a boil uncovered, then lower the heat and simmer for 1 1/2–2 hours. Soup will be thick and hearty. Serve with thick, crusty bread.

*To make it easier to remove the cloth, make the string long enough to tie around the handle of the soup pot.

PROJECT AND REPORT IDEAS

Maps

- Make a map of the eurozone, and create a legend to indicate key manufacturing industries throughout the EU.
- Create a map of Central Europe. Use different colors to indicate how political boundaries have changed in the region as the Slovene people were subject to different kinds of government.

Journal

- Imagine you are on vacation in Slovenia. What cities and regions will you visit, and why? Describe the different people and places you encounter.
- The Ten Day War for Slovenian independence was brief and mostly bloodless, but people were still fearful about the future. Imagine you were a student during the Ten Day War. Write a journal entry describing your feelings about Slovenia becoming an independent country.

Reports

- Write a brief report on Slovene farming and the different crops produced.
- Write a brief report on the impact of EU membership on Slovenia.
- Write a brief report on how Slovenes were affected by any of the following historical events: World War I, World War II, the collapse of the Soviet Union.

Biographies
Write a one-page biography on one of the following:

- Josef Tito
- France Preseren
- Leon Stukelj

Projects

- Learn the Slovene expressions for simple words such as hello, good day, please, thank you. Try them on your friends.
- Make a calendar of your country's festivals and list the ones that are common or similar in Slovenia. Are they celebrated differently in Slovenia? If so, how?
- Make a poster to advertise Slovenian tourism.
- Make a list of all the rivers, places, seas, and islands that you have read about in this book and indicate them on a map of Slovenia.
- Find a Slovene recipe other than the ones given in this book, and ask an adult to help you make it. Share it with members of your class.

CHRONOLOGY

100 BCE	Romans begin to occupy Slovakia.
600 CE	Slavs fully inhabit the region.
788	Control of Slovene lands passes to the Franks.
962	Power is assumed by the Holy Roman Empire.
1335	Slovenia falls under Hapsburg rule.
1809	Napoleon occupies Slovenia.
1814	Hapsburgs regain control of the region.
1867	The Austro-Hungarian Empire is born.
1914	World War I begins.
1918	The "National Council" forms the Kingdom of Serbs, Croats, and Slovenes.
1929	The country is renamed the Kingdom of Yugoslavia.
1941	Nazi Germany annexes most of Slovenia.
1945	Josef Tito institutes a communist dictatorship to rule Yugoslavia.
1989	Slovene parliament asserts its right to secede from Yugoslavia.
1990	A referendum is passed overwhelmingly supporting Slovene independence.
1991	Slovenia separates from Yugoslavia and communist rule ends.
1990	Milan Kucan was democratically elected the first president of Slovenia.
2003	Slovenes pass a referendum supporting membership in the EU.
2004	Slovenia is admitted to the EU and NATO.

FURTHER READING/INTERNET RESOURCES

Benderly, Jill, and Evan Kraft. *Independent Slovenia: Origins, Movements, Prospects.* New York: Palgrave Macmillan, 1996.

Carmichael, Cathie, and James Gow. *Slovenia and the Slovenes.* Bloomington: Indiana University Press, 2000.

Ferfila, Bogomil, and Paul Phillip. *Slovenia: On the Edge of the European Union.* Lanham, Md.: University Press of America, 2000.

Mrak, Mojmir, and Matija Rojec. *Slovenia: From Yugoslavia to the European Union.* Herndon, Va.: World Bank Publications, 2004.

Orr, Tamra. *Slovenia.* New York: Scholastic Library Publishing, 2004.

Sinkovek, Bostjan. *Cornerstones of Slovenia's NATO Membership.* Lincoln, Neb.: iUniverse Inc., 2003.

Travel Information
www.lonelyplanet.com/destinations/europe/slovenia/
www.randburg.com/si

History and Geography
www.world infozone.com/country.php?country=slovenia
www.answers.com/topic/history-of-slovenia

Culture and Festivals
www.sloveniainfo.com
www.uvi.si/sydney2000/eng/slovenia/culture
www.matkurja.com

Economic and Political Information
www.cia.gov/cia/publications/factbook/index.html
www.encyclopedia.com/html/section/slovenia_landpeopleandeconomy.asp

EU Information
europa.eu.int/

Publisher's note:
The Web sites listed on this page were active at the time of publication. The publisher is not responsible for Web sites that have changed their addresses or discontinued operation since the date of publication. The publisher will review and update the Web-site list upon each reprint.

For More Information

Embassy of the Republic of Slovenia
1525 New Hampshire Avenue
Washington, DC, 20036
Tel.: 202-667-5363
Fax: 202-667-4563

Slovenian Tourist Information Centre
Krekov trg 10
SI-1000 Ljubljana
Slovenia
Tel.: 386 (1) 306-4575
Fax: 386 (1) 306-4580

Embassy of the United States in Slovenia
Presernova 31
1000 Ljubljana
Slovenia
Tel.: 386 (1) 200-5500
Fax: 386 (1) 200-5555

European Union
Delegation of the European Commission to the United States
2300 M Street, NW
Washington, DC 20037
Tel.: 202-862-9500
Fax: 202-429-1766

annexed: Took over a territory and incorporated it into another political territory.

arable: Capable of being cultivated for growing crops.

authoritarian: Favoring strict rules and established authority.

autonomous: Able to act independently.

autonomy: Political independence and self-government.

blocs: United groups of countries.

bureaucracy: An administrative system in which work is divided into specific categories and carried out by special departments.

capital: Wealth in the form of money or property.

Celts: An ancient Indo-European people who lived in pre-Roman central and western Europe.

chamois: An agile goat antelope.

codified: Arranged into an organized system.

collective presidency: Governance where more than one person shares a single position of power.

communists: Supporters of the political and social theory in which all property of a classless society is owned by all the members of the community.

conifers: Trees that have thin leaves (needles) and produces cones.

conservation: The preservation, management, and care of natural and cultural resources.

deciduous: Term used to describe trees or shrubs that shed their leaves in the fall.

Eastern Bloc: The group of Eastern European countries with a shared aim.

ecotourists: Tourists who attempt to minimize ecological damage to the areas they visit.

elite: A small group of people within a larger group who have more power, prestige, wealth, or talent than the rest of the group.

excise: A type of tax on domestic goods.

feudal system: The legal and social system that existed in medieval Europe, in which vassals held land from lords in exchange for military service.

Franks: Members of a Germanic people who lived along the Rhine valley in the fourth century CE.

glacial lakes: Lakes formed when a body of water is blocked by ice from a glacier, after the glacier first carves out the bowl for the water to collect.

homogeneous: Having a uniform composition or structure.

Illyrians: People who, from the later third century BCE, occupied the Adriatic coastal regions from Albania northward.

indigenous: Native to a region.

infrastructure: Large-scale public services and facilities necessary for economic activity.

insular: Concerned only with one's own country, society, or way of life.

Napoleonic Code: The first successful set of civil laws, formulated under Napoleon's rule of France.

nationalist: Someone with feelings of extreme devotion to one nation and its interests above all others.

neutral: Not belonging to or favoring any side in a dispute.

nobility: The select group of people possessing an aristocratic social position or rank.

parliament: A legislative body.

polenta: Cornmeal mush.

proximity: Nearness to something.

ratified: Officially approved.

reneged: Went back on a promise or commitment.

secede: Formally withdraw from an organization, state, or alliance.

solidarity: Standing together in a show of unity.

sovereignty: Supreme authority.

stagnancy: A state of inactivity.

strudels: Desserts made with thin pastry rolled and baked with a filling, usually fruit.

tariff: A tax levied by a government on goods, usually imports.

temperate: A range of moderate climate conditions.

thermal springs: Water that flows from inside the earth, heated by the earth's interior warmth.

tidal estuaries: The lower courses of rivers where the tide flows in and fresh and salt water mix.

INDEX

PICTURE CREDITS

Biographies

Author

Heather Docalavich first developed an interest in the history and cultures of Eastern Europe through her work as a genealogy researcher. She currently resides in Hilton Head, South Carolina, with her four children.

Series Consultant

Ambassador John Bruton served as Irish Prime Minister from 1994 until 1997. As prime minister, he helped turn Ireland's economy into one of the fastest-growing in the world. He was also involved in the Northern Ireland Peace Process, which led to the 1998 Good Friday Agreement. During his tenure as Ireland's prime minister, he also presided over the European Union presidency in 1996 and helped finalize the Stability and Growth Pact, which governs management of the euro. Before being named the European Commission Head of Delegation in the United States, he was a member of the convention that drafted the European Constitution, signed October 29, 2004.

The European Commission Delegation to the United States represents the interests of the European Union as a whole, much as ambassadors represent their countries' interests to the U.S. government. Matters coming under European Commission authority are negotiated between the commission and the U.S. administration.